Ready, Set, Cheer!

CHEERLEADING BASICS

LISA MULLARKEY

E | **Enslow Publishers, Inc.**
40 Industrial Road
Box 398
Berkeley Heights, NJ 07922
USA

http://www.enslow.com

Many thanks to Emily Beggiato, Erika Lipinski, Alyssa Materazzo,
Abby Michta, Sarah Mullarkey, and Bryanna Papcun
for their contributions to this book.

Library of Congress Cataloging-in-Publication Data

Mullarkey, Lisa.
    Cheerleading basics / Lisa Mullarkey.
       p. cm. — (Ready, set, cheer!)
    Includes bibliographical references and index.
    Summary: "Readers will learn about the history of cheerleading, spirit, spirit sticks, bags,
stretching and gear, hand, arm, and leg motions, jumps, chants, and cheers"—Provided by
publisher.
    ISBN 978-0-7660-3536-2
    1. Cheerleading—Juvenile literature. I. Title.
    LB3635.M84 2010
    791.6'4—dc22
                      2009037240

ISBN-13: 978-1-59845-198-6 (paperback)

Printed in the United States of America

10 9 8 7 6 5 4 3 2 1

052010 Lake Book Manufacturing, Inc., Melrose Park, IL

To Our Readers: We have done our best to make sure all Internet addresses in this book were active
and appropriate when we went to press. However, the author and the publisher have no control over
and assume no liability for the material available on those Internet sites or on other Web sites they
may link to. Any comments or suggestions can be sent by e-mail to comments@enslow.com or to the
address on the back cover.

♻ Enslow Publishers, Inc., is committed to printing our books on recycled paper. The paper in every
book contains 10% to 30% post-consumer waste (PCW). The cover board on the outside of each book
contains 100% PCW. Our goal is to do our part to help young people and the environment too!

CONTENTS

1. *Shout It Out!* 5

2. *Bring It On!* 15

3. *Motions* 19

4. *Jumps* 29

5. *Chants and Cheers* 34

Words to Know 44

*Learn More: Books and
   Web Sites* 46

Index 48

Cheerleaders at Ohio State University form a pyramid.

1 SHOUT IT OUT!

Does your heart skip a beat when cheerleaders do daring stunts? Are you impressed by their leaps and tumbles? Do the dance moves get your feet tapping? If cheerleaders pump you up, maybe you need to jump out of the stands and into a squad!

Today's cheerleaders are athletes. Athletes are people trained in a sport. Cheerleaders are strong like football players. They have the energy of soccer players. Their focus must be like baseball players'. They are as flexible as gymnasts. Cheerleaders must also be agile like tennis players. (*Agile* means able to move fast and with ease.) How can anyone argue that cheerleading is not a sport?

But cheerleading is not *just* a sport. It is a way of thinking. Do you have what it takes to succeed?

★ *Are you a hard worker?* Cheerleaders make it look easy. Do not be fooled! It takes as much practice as any other sport.

★ *Do you have a winning attitude?* Cheerleaders don't give up.

★ *Are you a team player?* There is no "I" in TEAMWORK!

★ *Are you a good sport* even when you lose?

★ *Can you accept constructive criticism* from your coach and your peers?

Cheerleading is a fun way to spend time with friends, but it is also hard work.

If you answered yes to all of the above, becoming a cheerleader may be right for you! There are lots of places for you to cheer. Does your school have a squad? Is there an all-star team in your area? All-stars do not cheer for teams. They compete against other squads. You must try out for an all-star team. Many towns have teams where there are no tryouts. Everyone makes the team. With so many choices, the perfect team is waiting for you!

SIMPLY BECAUSE WE DO NOT RUN ACROSS GOAL LINES, SLAM-DUNK BASKETBALLS, OR HIT HOME RUNS DOESN'T MEAN WE CAN'T CHANGE THE SCORE.

Why Cheer?

Cheerleading is good for you! Besides providing you with exercise, cheering can increase your confidence. You will feel great about your healthy body. You will feel proud of your dedication to a sport. It builds friendships and good character. You will learn to be a team player. Your leadership skills will grow. So, get ready to shout it out and join the millions of kids who cheer today!

The History of Cheerleading

Cheering for a favorite competitor most likely started at the first Olympic Games in ancient Greece. In America, a student at Princeton University in New Jersey shouted the first cheer at a football game. That was in 1884. The cheer was simple: "Sis boom rah!"

A few years later, Johnny Campbell started the first organized team, at the University of Minnesota. He was called a yell leader. He started "yelling" because the football team was bad. He thought they needed cheering up *and* cheering on! Even with the cheers and chants, the football team lost a lot. But thanks to Campbell, cheerleading spread across the country.

At first, cheerleaders used simple chants, cheers, and signs to get the crowds going. In 1920, teams added gymnastics

In the beginning, only boys were cheerleaders. This picture is from a 1929 movie, *The Sophomore*.

Franklin D. Roosevelt

FIVE OF OUR PRESIDENTS WERE CHEERLEADERS!

1. **Franklin D. Roosevelt**
2. **Dwight D. Eisenhower**
3. **Ronald Reagan**
4. **George Bush**
5. **George W. Bush**

George W. Bush

and tumbling to the cheers, which made them much more exciting to watch. Until 1923, only men were cheerleaders. Although some women joined teams after that, there were not many. When men went off to fight in World War II, women were needed for the squads. Ever since then, there have been more women than men who cheer.

In the 1940s, Lawrence Herkimer founded the National Cheerleaders Association. He held clinics to help cheerleaders learn the basics. He worked hard to make sure kids were safe and he tried to convince people that cheerleading was a sport. He invented the pom-pom and has a jump—the Herkie—named after him.

In the 1960s, the Baltimore Colts football team had the first professional cheering squad. In 1978, college competitions were on TV for the first time. The first basket toss was done in competition, too. A basket toss is an advanced stunt. A cheerleader is tossed high into the air. She is called a *flyer* because she soars through the air. The flyer lands in a cradle position in the arms of the cheerleaders who tossed her. They are called *bases*. A base is a cheerleader who throws, lifts, or holds a cheerleader in the air during a stunt.

In the 1980s, some people said that cheerleading was getting too dangerous. The stunts were too risky. Rules were

These young women at the University of Nebraska were among the first female cheerleaders during the 1920s. Since World War II, more girls than boys have been cheerleaders.

made to protect cheerleaders from getting hurt. Cheerleading became more popular than ever. Competitions increased and gyms started forming all-star squads.

In 1995, the first cheerleading magazine was published. In 1999, ESPN (a TV sports network) agreed with cheerleaders that cheerleading was a sport. Cheerleaders were thrilled but wondered what took them so long.

Cheerleading in the 2000s continues to grow. Camps and clinics are part of a cheerleader's life. The cheers get louder. The stunts get harder. The tumbles get faster. The jumps get higher. Cheerleaders would not have it any other way!

Show Your Spirit!

All cheerleaders have spirit, but what is it? Spirit is pride in your team, school, and yourself. You can feel it. It is that burst of energy that whips through the air. You can hear it. It is the buzz in the locker room before the game. It is the chatter in the stands during the competition. You can see it. Look into

A team mascot helps get the crowd energized at a game. The Bruin is the UCLA mascot.

11

the stands. Are people dressed in your team's colors? Is your mascot making kids laugh? Your job as a cheerleader is to help spread the spirit with your positive attitude.

Spirit Stick

In 1954, Lawrence "Herkie" Herkimer, who started the National Cheerleaders Association, held a cheerleading camp. He gave out awards to teams who had the best jumps, stunts, and tumbling. But the team that impressed him most was not

A spirit stick

as good as the other squads. Their jumps were not high. Their tumbles and stunts were not strong. But they had something that no other team had: a spirit that could not be broken. They cheered other teams on. They worked harder than other teams. Smiles never left their faces. Herkie knew they would not get an award for their skills. But he felt they deserved something for their spirit. He snapped a twig off of a tree and told them that they had won the first ever *spirit stick*. A new tradition started!

Today, coaches award the spirit stick after a practice or game to the cheerleader who had a winning attitude. She keeps the stick until the next game or practice. Before it is returned, she writes her name on it and adds a small trinket (a sticker or charm) to it. By the end of the season, the spirit stick will look very different.

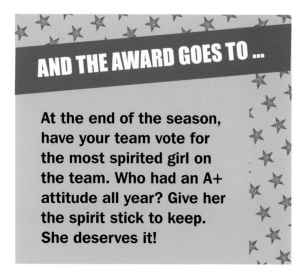

AND THE AWARD GOES TO ...

At the end of the season, have your team vote for the most spirited girl on the team. Who had an A+ attitude all year? Give her the spirit stick to keep. She deserves it!

Make a Spirit Stick

Use an empty potato chip can or a paper towel roll. Roll and glue felt around it to cover it. Use your team colors. Add beads or beans inside to make noise. Cover the ends with small pom-poms. Your spirit stick is ready!

Spirit Bags

Here is a fun idea to start the season off right. Decorate a brown paper lunch bag in your team colors. Use markers or paint. Punch holes in the bag and push ribbons through it to make streamers. Put the following items in the bag. Add a note to explain what each object stands for.

★ *Paper snowflake:* Everyone is special and unique.

★ *Star:* You shine and should reach for the stars.

★ *Penny:* You are a valuable part of the team.

★ *Gold thread:* Our friendship and spirit ties our hearts together.

★ *Pipe cleaner:* Stretch to stay flexible.

★ *Eraser:* We all make mistakes.

★ *Puzzle piece:* The squad would not be complete without you.

★ *Happy-face sticker:* Smile, smile, smile!

★ *Sponge:* Soak up the coach's tips.

★ *Popsicle stick:* Stick together through good and bad times.

★ *Rubber band:* Snap your motions!

★ *Balloon:* Keep spirits inflated.

★ *Glove:* Give someone a helping hand when needed.

2 BRING IT ON!

Cheerleaders use their entire bodies to perform, so it is important for them to be in tip-top shape. Stretch before practices and games. It will keep your body flexible. Stretching is a simple exercise that will help prevent muscles from getting hurt. Coaches are trained to know which stretching exercises are best for you. They will develop a plan for your team that will strengthen your upper and lower body muscles. Your coach will introduce the following stretches to you: hamstring, shoulder, canoe, back arm lift, calf, squats, lunges, straddles, toe touches, diamond, and beauty queen.

Be sure to watch closely when your coach demonstrates the proper way to stretch. If you stretch at home, do not bounce up and down. Take it slow. It is not a race.

Cheer Gear

Cheerleaders do not need a lot of fancy equipment or clothes. Your uniform will most likely be a skirt and a snug-fitting top. Sneakers are a must. Your coach will tell you which ones are safe for cheering. Everyone will wear the same style socks, too. Cheerleaders need to think about the safety of others.

Most cheerleading uniforms consist of a short skirt and snug-fitting top.

Stretching helps keep your body flexible and prevent injuries.

Remember the following safety tips:

★ *Pull* your hair back.

★ *Do not chew* gum.

★ *Do not wear jewelry*—it could scratch someone.

★ *Keep your fingernails trimmed* to avoid scratching yourself and your teammates.

★ *Wear snug-fitting clothes* so others can grab onto you easily.

Some squads use *pom-poms* to attract the crowd's attention. They show off moves while cheering or dancing. They are colored balls made of plastic or paper. Pom-poms are often used in the beginning of a routine and then tossed to the ground so the cheerleader's hands are free for stunting.

POM-POM POWER!

The first pom-poms were made out of paper. They were hard to take care of. The colors faded and the paper fell out. Today, pom-poms are made out of plastic. They are also called pom-pons.

When you get your first set of pom-poms, you will need to fluff them up. It takes about fifteen minutes to fluff each one. Lay your poms on a table. Look under the handle. You will see two sides of a pom. Start with one side. Lift a strand up and pull it to the right. Pull the next one up and to the left. Do this until both sides on both poms are fluffy.

3 MOTIONS

Cheerleaders use their bodies all the time to get the crowd excited. It is important to master hand, arm, and leg movements first. These are called *motions*. They are the basics of cheerleading. All cheerleading chants and cheers start with these motions.

All motions (every clap, jump, and stunt) need to be sharp and quick. Do not throw your legs and arms out into the air. Use your muscles to control where they go. If you do not practice your motions, you will look sloppy. Squads with sloppy motions look lazy.

Sharp and Snappy Makes Coaches Happy!

Look into a mirror or videotape yourself so you can see what your motions look like. Watch your posture and keep your head up. Look out at the crowd, not at the ground. Stand

Motions are the hand, leg, and arm movements cheerleaders use.

with your feet together. Clasp your arms behind your back. Use short, snappy movements to go from one motion to the other. It makes your chant look polished.

Practice in your room. Practice at the bus stop. Practice makes perfect! Once you nail the motions, the fun begins! You will be able to mix and match them to create new cheers and chants in no time.

A GOOD CHEERLEADER IS NOT MEASURED BY THE HEIGHT OF HER JUMPS BUT BY THE SPAN OF HER SPIRIT.

Hand Positions

There are five basic hand positions. You will use them in every chant and cheer. They are *blades, buckets, candlesticks, daggers,* and *knockers.*

★ *Blades:* Your fingers and thumbs are out straight. Your hand is flat. Your thumb must face forward.

You need to make a fist for the remaining hand motions. Your thumb must always stay on the outside. Do not tuck it under your fingers. If you do, your thumb could get hurt.

★ *Buckets:* Make fists. Your thumbs will face the ground. (Imagine that you are carrying a bucket by the handle.)

★ *Candlesticks:* Make fists and turn them so your thumbs face each other. (Imagine that you are

This is the hand position called *daggers.*

carrying a candle in each hand.)

★ *Daggers:* Make fists. Your pinky fingers should face forward toward the crowd. (Imagine holding a dagger in each hand, ready to thrust.)

★ *Knockers:* Make fists with your thumbs facing outward, toward the crowd. (Imagine that you are about to knock on a door.)

The Clap: Something to Applaud!

We clap all the time to show people we like something. But when cheerleaders clap, it is to help people. They clap to highlight certain parts of chants and cheers. It helps keep the beat. There are two claps cheerleaders must know.

★ *Basic clap:* Put your hands into blades. Bring

your hand together in front of your chest so your palms are flat and touching. Clap away!

★ *Clasp:* Start off in clap position. Slide right hand toward you and left hand toward crowd. Wrap fingers around hands.

Whether you are clapping or clasping, make sure your hands are not in front of your face—you want everyone to see your smile!

These cheerleaders show the difference between a clap (on left) and clasp.

Arm Positions

You can use lots of different hand positions with arm positions. Mix them up! When you do the arm motions, make sure your wrists are straight. If they bend, they will look sloppy.

★ *T:* Both arms are straight out to the side.

★ *Broken T:* Bend arms at elbow. Fists will be at chest.

★ *High V:* Arms are straight up in the air in the shape of a V, about twice shoulder width apart. Hold fists so thumbs face outward, away from each other.

★ *Low V:* Arms are facing down in a V, about twice shoulder width apart. Hold fists so thumbs face inward, toward each other.

★ *Diagonal:* One arm is in high V, other arm in low V.

★ *High touchdown:* Both arms are straight up in air, palms facing each other.

★ *Low touchdown:* Both arms down at sides, thumbs facing inward next to thigh.

★ *High X:* Arms above head like a touchdown, but crossing each other.

★ *Low X:* Arms in low touchdown, but crossing each other.

★ *Number 1:* One hand on hip, one hand straight in air.

★ *Right L:* Left arm is straight up in the air. Right arm is out to the side.

★ *Left L:* Right arm is straight up in the air. Left arm is out to the side.

★ *Right K:* Right hand in high V position. Left hand crosses body; thumb faces down.

★ *Left K:* Left hand in high V position. Right hand crosses body; thumb faces down.

Leg Positions

There are two basic leg positions: feet together and feet apart. In both, your legs are straight. Do not bend your knees. For feet apart, your feet should be slightly more than shoulder width apart. *Lunges* are popular, too. Step forward with one leg and bend your knee. Keep the other leg straight. Make up chants with both left- and right-leg lunges.

Feet apart

Feet together

In a lunge, the front leg is bent and the back leg is straight.

Kicks are fun to put into your cheers, chants, and stunts. The higher the kick, the more exciting it is to watch. When you kick, keep your back straight. One leg should be firmly on the ground and straight as possible while the leg in the air should be totally straight. Try to keep your toes pointed. Kicking takes lots of practice. It is easy to lose your balance. Do not forget to stretch before you kick.

The higher the kick, the more exciting it is to watch.

SHOP SMART

Cheering can get expensive! Many cheerleading squads raise money by selling clothes with their team logo and colors. While these clothes are fun to wear, you do not need them to be a good cheerleader. If you really want something, try to save money or earn it.

4

JUMPS

Cheerleaders love to show off their jumps! It adds excitement to chants and cheers. Sometimes everyone in the squad jumps at the same time. The timing has to be perfect. Everyone must be on the same part of the jump at the same time. That is tough to do. Some cheers or dances have cheerleaders jump after each other but within seconds of one another. When this happens, it is like fireworks exploding into the air. Jumping is hard work. You need strong muscles. You need to be flexible and in good shape. You use every part of your body to jump. Spend time stretching all of your muscles before practicing your jumps.

When you first learn your jumps, you will use a *spotter*. Spotters are people who already knows the motions. They will guide you through the jump. They may hold onto

Jumps add excitement to chants and cheers.

your waist and help you get up higher. They will stand behind you and catch you if you start to fall.

There are lots of jumps you can learn. All jumps have three parts: prep, lift, and landing. You must do all three parts for your jump to be a success.

Prep—short for "preparation"—is the first step. It helps you get the power you need to get your feet off of the ground. Stand with your legs together and your arms at your sides. Bring your arms up into a high V motion while lifting on your toes. Swing both arms down and across your body. When arms are at their lowest point, bend your knees a bit. Use your knees and toes to push off. This pushing off is your lift. At the same time as your liftoff, your arms will go back up to a high V. Your arms and legs will now form the jump. When you have hit your position and cannot go any higher,

RISKY BUSINESS?

Recent studies have shown that cheerleading can be a dangerous sport. New rules and better training for coaches are aimed at making cheerleading less risky. You need to play a part in preventing injuries by listening carefully to you coaches and following their instructions to the letter. Cheerleaders also need to pay attention to each other and look out for risky situations. Following the rules isn't just a good idea—it can keep you safe.

In a toe touch jump, it's important for the arms and legs to be straight.

put your legs together and land. Bend your knees when you land. Land on the balls of your feet. The ball of your foot is the soft part right behind your toes. You may want to add a high V or another arm motion after you land.

Try these jumps. Remember to start with the prep.

★ *Tuck:* Pull your knees up to your chest. Hold your hands in a high V.

★ *Toe touch:* Lift you legs as high as you can into a splits position. Lean forward at your waist. Keep your head up and face your shoulders forward. Your arms are in a low V position (or T position).

★ *Herkie:* Bring your arms into a Number One motion. Lift your front leg straight out to the side with your knee facing up. Bend the other leg behind your body and point your knee down. Keep your back straight and toes pointed.

5
CHANTS AND CHEERS

Cheerleaders use chants and cheers to impress the fans at a game. Some are short to help keep things moving during time-outs or breaks. Others are longer and used at halftime.

Whether you are cheering or chanting, you will be performing in front of a crowd. Your voice should be loud and clear. Everyone should be able to hear you. It is important to *project* your voice. It must travel from where you are to the very last row in the stands. How can you do this? Do not scream. Instead, pretend your voice is like a bow and arrow. Help your voice sail through the air and hit the target in the back row.

To help you project your voice, take breaths from your diaphragm instead of your chest. Your diaphragm is a muscle used for breathing. It is below the rib cage, and it separates the chest cavity from the abdomen. Use your diaphragm to push out your cheers.

Do not forget to *enunciate*! Enunciate means to speak clearly. Do not let your words run together. If you do, no one will understand the words in your chants or cheers. Speak slowly and say each word with power. Stress each syllable (part) of a word in a chant.

These high school cheerleaders in Connecticut use a chant to inspire fans at a football game.

PROJECTION PERFECTION

To practice projecting your voice, lie flat on your back with your legs up in the air. Say a cheer. You will be able to feel the words coming from your diaphragm.

Try this out: Say the word *hello* in your normal voice. Now pick a target across the room. Can you get your voice over there? Say it again, but shout it out like you would on the playground. You probably sucked in a breath and shouted from your chest. If you do this while cheering, your voice will get tired and hoarse.

Now repeat *hello* but take a deep breath from your diaphragm below your chest. Speak when you exhale (let your breath out). Your hello will be louder!

Chants

A chant is a short, peppy cheer. It is repeated several times. Arm and leg motions emphasize the beat of the words. Chants are catchy and easy to remember. If you are loud enough, the crowd will chant with you.

The first time you lead a chant, you might feel shy. Here are some tips to help you boost your confidence and get the crowd chanting with you.

1. Smile! If you smile at the crowd, they will smile back at you.

2. Move around. Act confident. Do not stand in one place for too long.

Cheerleaders often don't have megaphones to help them project their voices. They need to learn how to be loud and clear.

3. Point into the crowd and ask, "Are you ready to cheer?" When they respond "Yes," say, "Louder." They will respond "Yes" louder. This will make more people pay attention to you.

4. Have your pom-poms in your hands. This will help people spot you easily.

5. Keep it short and simple.

UCLA cheerleaders welcome the crowd with a cheer.

This is a perfect crowd chant:

Point pom-poms at yourself and chant:
"We say Princeton."

Point pom-poms at them:
"You say Tigers."

Point pom-poms back at yourself:
"Princeton"

Point pom-poms back at them:
"Tigers"

Point pom-poms back at yourself:
"We say orange."

Point pom-poms back at them:
"You say black."

Point pom-poms back at yourself:
"Orange."

Point pom-poms back at them:
"Black"

Repeat this at least three times. It will fire up the crowd! (You will want to use your own town or team nickname and mascot along with your colors.)

Here are some more chants. Can you make up some motions to go with them? Then make up chants of your own!

Stand up
It's time to shout
Come on fans
Yell it out
Say it loud
Say it proud
Go, fight, win!
Check out the score
(Team name) want more
We ain't needy
We're just greedy!

For football:

First and ten
Let's do it again!

For basketball:

Genie! Genie!
Grant our wish!
Genie! Genie!
Swish, swish, swish!

Cheers

Cheers are longer than chants. Stunting, dancing, and tumbling are involved. You must practice them over and over again. There are lots of words and actions to remember.

"Hello" cheers are popular. It is the first cheer you do to welcome everyone.

Cheerleaders perform during halftime at a basketball game.

Hello! How are you? How do you do?
(Team name) welcome you.
Sit back. Relax.
You've seen us before.
But now we're back to raise the score.
(Now individual cheerleaders introduce themselves and do a
jump of their choice.)
My name is _____(jump)
(After everyone has jumped, all shout "Welcome!")

Now that you have learned the basics of cheerleading, practice every day. Go find the perfect squad for you. As they say in cheerleading, bring it on! May the spirit of cheerleading be with you!

IT IS NOT THE GLITZ OF THE UNIFORM THAT MATTERS, BUT THE SPIRIT THAT SHINES WITHIN IT.

WORDS TO KNOW

all-star teams—Squads of cheerleaders who compete with other squads instead of cheering for a sports team.

base—A cheerleader who throws, lifts, or holds another in the air during a stunt.

chant—A short, peppy cheer, repeated several times.

enunciate—To speak clearly.

flyer—A cheerleader who is lifted or thrown into the air.

Herkie—A jump named for Lawrence Herkimer, who started the American Cheerleaders Association.

mascot—A costumed character or animal that represents a sports team. Mascots appear at games to encourage team spirit.

motions—Hand, arm, and leg movements that are the basis of all cheers.

pom-poms—Fluffy, colored balls made out of plastic or paper.

prep (short for "preparation")—The movements a cheerleader makes to get ready for a jump or stunt.

spotter—Someone who guides another cheerleader through a jump or stunt to make sure he or she does not get hurt.

stunt—An activity that involves lifting or throwing a cheerleader.

LEARN MORE

BOOKS

Gruber, Beth. *Cheerleading for Fun!* Minneapolis: Compass Point Books, 2004.

Jones, Jen. *Cheer Basics: Rules to Cheer By.* Mankato, Minn.: Capstone Press, 2006.

Maurer, Tracy Nelson. *Competitive Cheerleading.* Vero Beach, Fla.: Rourke Publishing, 2006.

Valliant, Doris. *The History of Cheerleading.* Philadelphia: Mason Crest Publishers, 2003.

WEB SITES

Activity TV: Cheerleading
<http://www.activitytv.com/cheerleading-for-kids>

American Youth Football and Cheer
<http://www.americanyouthfootball.com/
cheerleading.asp>

Varsity Official Site
<http://www.varsity.com/>

INDEX

A
agile, 5
all-star team, 7, 11
arm positions, 24–25
athlete, 5

B
Baltimore Colts, 10
bases, 10
basket toss, 10

C
Campbell, Johnny, 8
chant, 8, 19, 21, 22, 26, 28, 29, 34, 35, 36, 38–39, 41
cheer, 8, 21, 22, 28, 29, 34, 35, 36, 42–43
cheerleading camp, 11, 12
cheerleading clinic, 9, 11
clap, 19, 22–23

D
diaphragm, 34–35, 36

E
enunciate, 35
ESPN, 11

F
flyer, 10

G
Greece, 7

H
hand positions, 19, 21–22, 24
Herkie, the, 9, 33
Herkimer, Lawrence, "Herkie", 9, 12, 13

J
jump, 11, 12, 19, 29, 31, 33

K
kick, 28

L
leg position, 26
lunge, 15, 26

M
motions, 19, 21, 24, 29, 31, 33, 36

N
National Cheerleaders Association, 9

O
Olympic Games, 7

P
pom-pom, 9, 13, 18, 38, 39
practice, 6, 19, 21, 28, 36, 42, 43
prep, 31, 33
project, 34, 36
Princeton University, 8

S
safety, 16–17, 31
spirit, 11, 12
spirit bag, 13–14
spirit stick, 12–13
spotter, 29
stretch, 15, 28, 29
stunt, 10, 11, 12, 18, 19, 42

T
teamwork, 6

U
uniform, 16
University of Minnesota, 8